PUMPKINS

PUMPKINS

MetroBooks

MetroBooks

An Imprint of Friedman/Fairfax Publishers

ISBN 1-58663-065-2

Introduction by Rynn Williams
Editor: Susan Lauzau
Art Director: Jeff Batzli
Designer: Millie Sensat
Photography Editor: Sarah Storey
Production Director: Karen Matsu Greenberg

Color separations by Colourscan Pte Ltd.
Printed in Singapore by KHL Printing Co. Ltd.

1 3 5 7 9 10 8 6 4 2

For bulk purchases and special sales, please contact:
Friedman/Fairfax Publishers
Attention: Sales Department
15 West 26th Street
New York, NY 10010
212/685-6610 FAX 212/685-1307

Visit our website:
www.metrobooks.com

Dense, richly hued, as sensuous as sculpture,

pumpkins never fail to summon images of a

crisp and dazzling autumn…

—Rynn Williams

The robust, tough-skinned, golden pumpkin—a harbinger of winter's chill yet as warm and friendly as the October sun—what could be a better emblem of the mercurial autumn season? Dense, richly hued, as sensuous as sculpture, these versatile vine-ripened fruits clustered at a roadside farm stand never fail to summon images of a crisp and dazzling autumn—red barns, white fences, and startling blue skies. They summon memories of childhood perhaps, from cheery, flickering faces of jack-o'-lanterns on the windowsill to holiday tables laden with fresh-baked desserts. As the quintessential American poet John Greenleaf Whittier once wrote: "What moistens the lip and brightens the eye? What calls back the past, like the rich Pumpkin Pie?"

But this fruit, which has long been a symbol of bountiful harvests and celebration, also has a dark side: when pumpkins appear, goblins, ghouls, witches, and the long dark nights of winter lie just around the corner.

The name pumpkin springs from the Greek *pepon*, or large melon. As part of the vast Cucurbitaceae family, the rotund ribbed fruit is related to melons as well as such seemingly disparate siblings as the cucumber and chayote. The English name *pumpkin*, which appeared in the 1640s, evolved from the sixteenth-century words *pompion* and *pumpion*.

But long before European settlers were introduced to the pumpkin, variations on these native American fruits were crucial to the pre-Colombian diet of the Aztecs and others. Remains of pumpkinlike seeds dating as far back as 7000 to 5000 B.C. have been found in remote caves in Mexico's Tamaulipas mountains. Spanish explorers noted that natives in South America consumed various strains of a pumpkinlike fruit. *Pepian*, a delicious pumpkin-seed sauce, is still a rich Guatemalan delicacy, and in the Andes a pumpkin stew is often served at Christmas.

Further up the globe, the Narragansett Indians of what is now the northeastern United States called pumpkins and other gourds and squashes *askooot-asquash*. Food historians note that squash was probably the very first crop cultivated by Native Americans (the Pueblo Indians of the southwestern United States were cultivating it two thousand years ago, and probably long before that). Along with corn and beans, squash was part of the triad known as the "Three Sisters of Life." These three foods combined to create

a nutritionally complete diet for thousands of years; Native Americans across the continent ate the inner flesh, the seeds, and the blossoms of pumpkins and other gourds, and dried the hard outer shells to make bowls. (A precursor to the hollowed-out pumpkins used as soup tureens on modern tables.)

It was the Patuxent Squanto Indians who taught Pilgrim settlers how to plant pumpkin vines among their corn stalks, the vines serving as a deterrent to raccoons and other animals. It's often said that without pumpkins to eat, the Pilgrims might not have survived winter in their new home. At their first Thanksgiving celebration in 1621 they probably made a pumpkin pudding sweetened with maple syrup or honey. And they might have tossed back a few gourds-full of pumpkin ale.

While it's unlikely that the Pilgrims made pumpkin pie, they did come close when they filled a hollowed pumpkin shell with milk and baked it until the liquid was absorbed, making a creamy dish just right for spooning. Today, the warm, deep orange and brown hue of the pumpkin pie, and the familiar smell of nutmeg and cinnamon, remind us each year of just how much we have to be grateful for.

Pumpkins make a more playful, if slightly ominous, appearance during the Halloween season. Pumpkin vines begin to produce fruit in the early days of autumn. To celebrate All Saints' Eve, they are transformed from simple, beautiful fruits on the vine into complex and sometimes frightening visages alive with personality and the spark of a hidden flame.

The Halloween holiday itself can be traced to Ireland, where the first of these lanterns were made from rutabagas, potatoes, turnips, even beets, and placed in windows or by doors to scare away the spirits that were rumored to walk the earth

on that ominous night. One of these spirits, Stingy Jack, gave the carved pumpkin its name. Stingy Jack was too mean to get into heaven, yet so cunning that he tricked the Devil into promising he would never go to hell. With no place to go, he was doomed to wander the earth by night in an eternal search for a place to rest. His only light was a meager turnip that he fashioned into a lamp with a burning coal inside. "Jack of the Lantern" evolved into "jack-o'-lantern," and when Irish immigrants came to the United States they found

that pumpkins, which had been unavailable in Ireland, were much easier to carve than turnips or beets.

While it's usually the medium-sized fruits that are used for carving, pumpkins can range from the tiny white ornamental 'Baby Boo', which you can hold in the palm of your hand, to the enormous 'Atlantic Giant' variety, which has the distinction of providing us with the world's largest pumpkin, grown by Paula and Nathan Zehr in Lowville, New York, and weighing in at a whopping 1,061 pounds [482kg].

pumpkin that's easy to handle (3 to 5 pounds [1.5 to 2.5kg]) and sweet.

Pumpkins grow on trailing vines that bear broad rough leaves and are punctuated by yellow flowers and tendrils. The plants like sun, water, and lots of fertilizer, and it's best to get them into the ground around mid-April. Like all winter squashes, pumpkins need lots of space to grow, so make sure to give them a plot of their own. Place wooden boards underneath the maturing fruit to keep it from rotting on the vine. They're ready for harvest when they are deep orange, with hard rinds, and the vine is beginning to die. This is usually in late September or early October, but the harvested pumpkins should keep for several months, especially if stored in a cool dry place.

Since they're harvested only in the autumn months, the appearance of pumpkins on the agricultural scene is a reassuring signal of seasonal passage. We see a field of ripening pumpkins and immediately we're transported to a world of cool nights, bright harvest moons, crackling fires, and the warmth of family and friends. Even before they were shared with the world beyond North America, pumpkins were a cornerstone of the American diet, offering solace and solid nutrition, as well as a rosy blush of color in a season that presages often-cruel winters. They are truly a reason for giving thanks.

In between these extremes ranges everything from 'Jack be Little', the deeply ribbed miniature pumpkins that show up in shop windows and kitchen windowsills at summer's first flight, to the rather flat 'Rouge Vif d'Etampes', also known as the Cinderella pumpkin, which ranges in color from burnt orange to red, to the white-skinned and perfectly round 'Lumina', which can weigh in at 20 pounds [9.5kg]. Of course there's the all-important 'Small Sugar', for those who still make their pies from scratch and need a

Photo Credits